PEGGY PARISH

Costumes to Make

ILLUSTRATED BY LYNN SWEAT

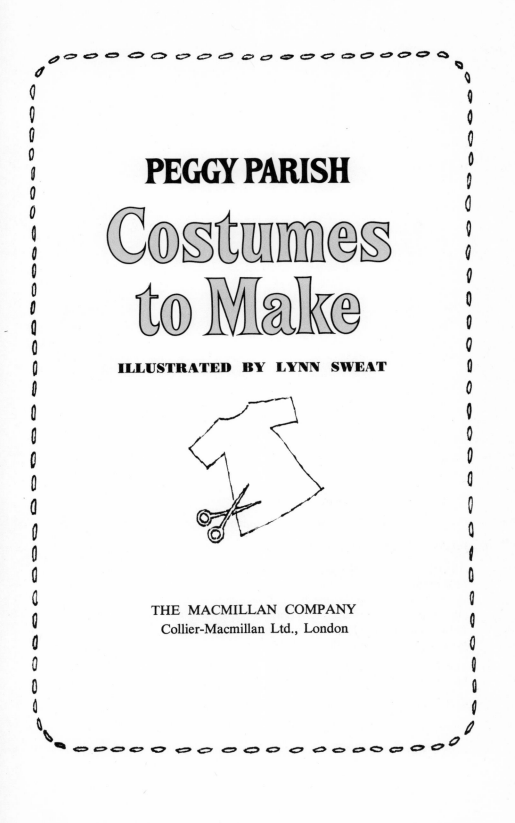

THE MACMILLAN COMPANY
Collier-Macmillan Ltd., London

For Carlye and Richard Selden
with love

J
646.4
P

Contents

INTRODUCTION

In making costumes it is the overall effect rather than the craftsmanship that is important.

This book will give you basic instructions for a number of different styles of costumes. But room is left for you to embellish them with any details you may wish to try.

The costumes for many story book characters are interchangeable. The ones in this book can be readily adapted for any number of other characters.

Many of these costumes call for a basic pattern, which means the essential parts of a commercial pattern without any of the novelty variations.

With other costumes you make your own paper pattern before cutting the fabric. Newspaper is ideal for this.

The terms "attach" and "bind" are frequently used in the instructions. To attach means to pin or baste before stitching. To bind means to encase the raw seam with bias tape or bias strips.

The long dresses will present a much more pleasing effect if they are worn over a crinoline or some other kind of full petticoat.

Costume making can be fun. So let your imagination run free and you may be surprised with your own ability to create.

Other Days, Other People

INDIAN BOY AND GIRL

Requirements: a fringed shirt or dress, fringed pants or leggings, and a headband. The boy's shirt should reach halfway to his knees. The girl's dress should reach below the knees.

Shirt and Dress

1. A loosefitting pajama jacket for boys and a robe for girls make good patterns. Place the buttoned jacket or robe on a double thickness of fabric. Cut around it, allowing a margin for seams. Cut a round neck.
2. Sew the shoulder and side seams.
3. Sew a line of stitching about three inches from the edge around the sleeves and the bottom.
4. Split the back of the neck three or four inches to make a head opening. Bind the neck.
5. Make fringe around the sleeves and the bottom by making cuts every half inch to the stitching line.
6. Crayon Indian designs on the front and the back.

Pants and Leggings

1. Use a basic pajama pants pattern for this. Follow the instructions given with the pattern for assembling.
2. Cut two strips of fabric about three inches wide and the length of the pants. At intervals of about one-half inch, make cuts about two and a half inches deep. Sew the fringe along the side of each pants leg.

Headband

1. Measure around the head and add one inch. Cut a strip of fabric that long and four inches wide.
2. Fold the fabric in half lengthwise and stitch. Turn and press.
3. Turn in the raw edges and sew the ends of the strip together.
4. Use either a real feather or one cut from paper. Staple or sew the feather in place at the back of the headband. Decorate the headband with Indian designs.

TURN AND PRESS

PURITAN GIRL

Requirements: a long-sleeved long dress, an apron, a white collar, and a cap.

Dress

1. Use any basic dress pattern with long sleeves. Cut the skirt the length you want it to be plus two inches for the hem. Follow the instructions given with the pattern for assembling.

Apron

1. Fold the fabric lengthwise with the selvages together. Measure the length you want the apron to be plus two inches for the hem. Cut along this line.
2. Gather the top edge of the apron.
3. For the waistband, cut a piece of fabric five inches shorter than the waist measurement and four inches wide.
4. Press a narrow hem along each side. Fold the band in half lengthwise and press.
5. Slip the skirt into the fold of the band and stitch in place.
6. Cut strips of fabric for ties and stitch down a narrow hem along each side. Attach the ties to the apron band and stitch in place. Hem the apron.

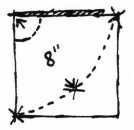

Collar

1. To make a pattern, measure eight inches from a corner of a folded sheet of paper to each point shown. Draw a curving line connecting these points. Cut along this line. Cut out a place for the neck.

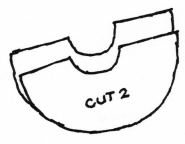

2. Keeping the pattern folded, cut enough from the end so that when opened the pattern is shaped as shown.

3. Using this pattern as a guide, cut two pieces from fabric.

4. Sew the pieces together as shown. Trim the seams, turn, and press.

5. Bind the neck with bias tape, allowing enough at each end to make ties.

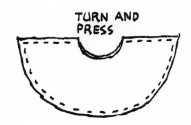

Cap

1. To make a pattern, cut a piece of paper ten inches wide and long enough to go around the head plus one inch. Round off the corners as shown. Cut it out.

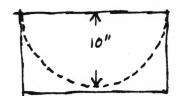

2. Using this as a guide, cut two pieces from fabric.

3. Sew the pieces together, leaving a small opening for turning. Trim the seams, turn, sew the opening, and press.

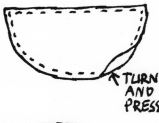

4. Fit the cap around the head. Sew the ends in place.

PURITAN BOY

Requirements: pants, a jacket, a white collar and cuffs, a hat, and knee socks. The knee socks are worn over the pants and tied in place with ribbon.

Pants and Jacket

1. Use a basic pajama pattern. Cut a round neck on the jacket. Follow the instructions given with the pattern for assembling. Leave jacket sleeves unhemmed.

Collar

1. To make a collar pattern, draw the neck and shoulder lines from the shirt front and back patterns on a sheet of paper. Measure the length so that the finished collar will be about seven inches deep from the shoulder to the bottom. Cut this out.

2. Using this as a guide, cut two back pieces and four front pieces from fabric. Sew each pair of fronts to a back at the shoulders. Sew the assembled pieces together except for the side seams. Trim the seams, turn, and press.

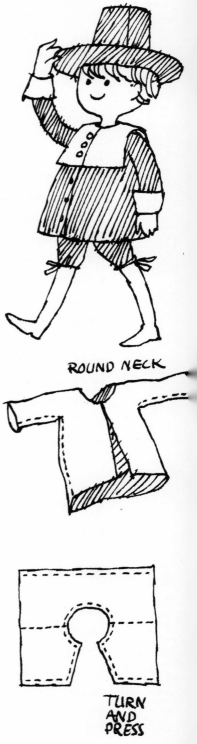

ROUND NECK

TURN AND PRESS

12

3. Turn under the raw edges and stitch together on the outside.

4. Make three buttonholes down the front. Sew on buttons.

Cuffs

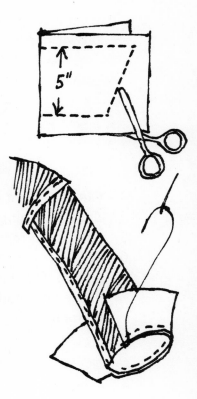

1. To make a pattern, measure the width of a jacket sleeve. Draw a line this length on a folded sheet of paper. Draw another line five inches above the first. Shape as shown. Cut it out and unfold.

2. Using this as a guide, cut four pieces from fabric.

3. Sew each pair together except at the bottom. Trim seams, turn, and press.

4. Attach the cuffs to the insides of the jacket sleeves, wrong sides facing, as shown. Stitch in place. Turn back over the sleeves and press.

Hat

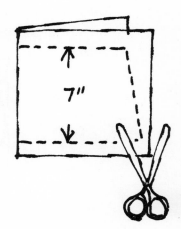

1. To make a pattern, measure around the head and add one inch. Draw a line half this length on a folded sheet of paper. Draw another line seven inches above the first. Shape the pattern as shown. Cut this out and unfold.

2. Using this as a guide, cut one piece from black fabric and one piece from brown paper.

3. Sew the sides of the fabric piece together.

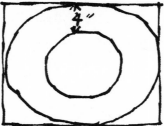

4. Cut a circle of fabric the same size as the top opening.

5. Attach the top to the sides as shown.

6. Sew the sides of the brown paper together. Fit this into the hat. Stitch paper and cloth together around the bottom.

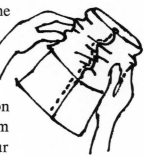

7. To make the brim, draw a circle on paper the same size as the bottom opening. Draw another circle four inches larger around the first. Cut as shown.

8. Using this as a guide, cut two circles from black fabric and one from brown paper.
9. Stitch the circles together with the brown paper in the middle.
10. Attach the brim to the crown as shown. Stitch in place.

FRONTIER BOY

Requirements: a fringed jacket, fringed pants, a knit shirt, and a coonskin hat.

Jacket and Pants

1. Use a basic pajama pattern. Cut a round neck on the jacket. Follow the instructions given with the pattern for assembling.
2. Cut long strips of fabric three inches wide. At intervals of about one-half inch make cuts two and a half inches deep to make the fringe. Sew the fringe along the side of each pants leg, the neck, the front, the bottom of the jacket, and the underside of each sleeve.

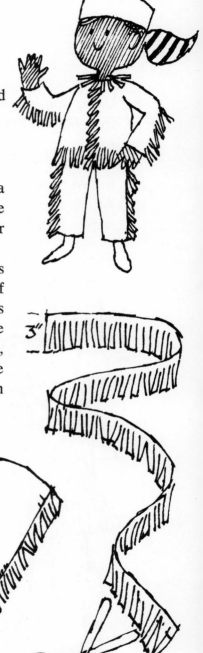

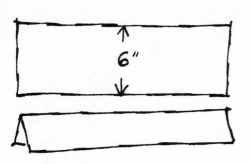

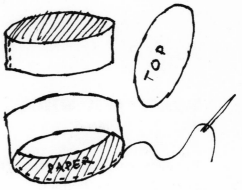

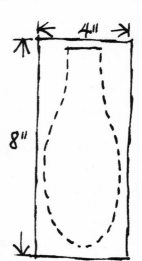

Coonskin Hat

1. Measure around the head and add one inch. Cut a strip of fabric that length and six inches wide. Cut a strip of brown paper that length and three inches wide.

2. Fold the fabric in half lengthwise and press.

3. Sew the ends together.

4. Cut a circle of fabric the same size as the top opening.

5. Attach the top to the crown. Stitch in place. Trim the seam and turn.

6. Fit the paper strip into the hat and stitch around the lower edge.

7. For the coon tail, cut two pieces of fabric eight inches long and four inches wide shaped as shown.

8. Sew the two pieces together except at the top. Trim the seams and turn.

9. Stuff the tail. Attach it to the underside of the hat. Hand stitch in place.

10. Paint on black stripes.

FRONTIER GIRL

Requirements: a long-sleeved long dress, an apron, and a bonnet.

Dress

1. Use any basic dress pattern with long sleeves. Cut the skirt the length you want it to be plus two inches for the hem. Follow the instructions given with the pattern for assembling.

Apron

1. Fold the fabric lengthwise with the selvages together. Measure the length you want the apron to be plus two inches for the hem. Cut along this line.
2. Gather the top edge of the apron.
3. For the waistband, cut a piece of fabric five inches shorter than the waist measurement and four inches wide.
4. Press a narrow hem along each side. Fold the band in half lengthwise and press.
5. Slip the skirt into the fold of the band and stitch in place.
6. Cut two pieces of fabric about eight inches wide and the height you want the bib to be. Sew the pieces together except at the bottom. Turn and press.

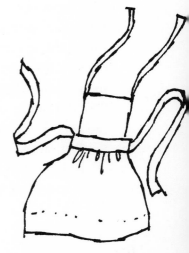

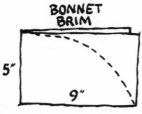

BONNET BRIM

5"

9"

7. Match the center of the bib to the center of the waistband. Stitch in place.

8. Cut ties for the waist and the neck. Turn under and stitch down a narrow hem along the edges. Attach to the apron as shown. Stitch in place. Hem the apron.

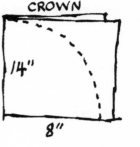

CROWN

14"

8"

Bonnet

1. To make a pattern, draw a line about nine inches long on a folded sheet of paper. Draw another line five inches above the first line. Shape as shown. Cut this out and unfold.

TURN AND PRESS

2. For the crown, draw a line fourteen inches high on a folded sheet of paper. Draw another line eight inches long. Join the lines as shown. Cut out and unfold.

3. Using these patterns as guides, cut out two pieces of fabric the shape of the brim and one of the crown.

4. Sew the brims together as shown. Trim the seams, turn, and press.

5. Gather the curved edge of the crown. Arrange the gathers and attach to the straight edge of the brim. Stitch in place.

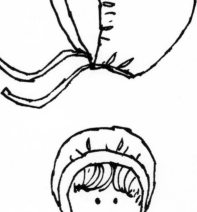

6. Gather the straight edge of the crown and bind, allowing enough binding at each end to tie under the chin.

OLD-FASHIONED BOY

Requirements: a dark coat with lots of buttons, a bright-colored vest, knee pants, a ruffled neckpiece, a tricorn hat, and white tights.

Coat

1. A basic robe pattern without the collar is good for this. Follow the instructions given with the pattern for assembling.
2. Cut a strip of fabric about two and a half inches wide and long enough to fit around the neck of the coat. Fold the strip in half lengthwise and sew the ends together. Turn and press.
3. Fit the strip around the neck of the coat, turning under a narrow hem along the edges. Attach and stitch.
4. For cuffs, cut two pieces of fabric about six inches wide and long enough to fit around the sleeves. Fold the pieces in half lengthwise and sew the ends together. Turn and press.
5. Fit the cuffs around the insides of the sleeves, wrong sides facing. Attach and stitch in place. Fold the cuffs back over the sleeve and press.
6. Put two buttons on each cuff.

Vest

1. The front and back pieces of a pajama coat pattern will make this. Cut two back pieces and four front pieces. Cut a V-shaped neck at the front.
2. Sew the two backs together except at the shoulders and sides. Turn and press. Do the same for each pair of fronts.
3. Sew the fronts to the back at the shoulder and side seams.
4. Make buttonholes and sew on buttons.

TURN
AND
PRESS

Ruffled Neckpiece

1. Cut a strip of fabric three inches wide and long enough to fit around the neck. Fold the strip in half lengthwise and stitch. Turn and press.
2. Cut a piece of fabric ten inches wide and eight inches long. Cut another piece ten inches wide and five inches long. Turn under a narrow hem on all sides and stitch.
3. Gather each piece at one end.
4. Sew the pieces to the neckband as shown.

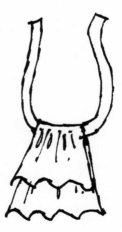

Knee Pants

1. A pajama pants pattern cut short will do for this. Follow the instructions given with the pattern for assembling. If you want the legs to fit tighter, insert a piece of elastic through the hems of each leg.

ELASTIC

Tricorn Hat

1. To make a pattern, measure around the head plus one inch. Draw a line half this length on paper. Cut along this line and shape the hat as shown.
2. Using this as a guide, cut two pieces from fabric.
3. Sew the curved edges together. Turn and press.
4. Cut a strip of fabric four inches wide and long enough to go around the bottom of the hat. Fold the strip lengthwise and shape the ends as shown.
5. Sew the ends, turn, and press.
6. Starting at the center front, fit the band to the inside of the crown. Attach and stitch. Fold the band back over the crown.

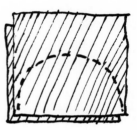

TURN
AND
PRESS

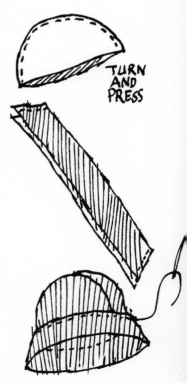

OLD-FASHIONED GIRL

Requirements: A long dress, a bonnet, and pantaloons.

Dress

1. Use any basic dress pattern. Measure the skirt length so that it will come about midway of the calf of the leg plus two inches for the hem. Follow the instructions given with the pattern for assembling.
2. Add lace or other trimming if you like.
3. For the sash, cut a strip of fabric five inches wide and long enough to go around the waist and tie in a big bow.
4. Turn under a narrow hem on all sides and stitch down.
5. Make loops on each side of the dress for the sash to pass through or tack the sash to the center front of the dress.

Bonnet

1. To make a pattern, draw a line on a folded sheet of paper about nine inches long. Draw another line nine inches above the first. Shape as shown.

2. Cut out and unfold the pattern. Using it as a guide, cut two pieces from fabric.

3. Sew the pieces together, leaving a small opening for turning. Trim the seams, turn, sew the opening, and press.

4. To make a ruffle, cut a strip of cloth three inches wide and thirty-six inches long.

5. Turn under a narrow hem on all sides and stitch down. Gather the strip along one edge. Attach the ruffle to the curved edge of the bonnet and stitch. Make ties and attach to each side of the bonnet.

Pantaloons

1. Use a basic pattern for pajama pants. Follow the instructions given with the pattern for assembling.

2. Make ruffles as for the bonnet. Sew three or four rows of ruffles to each pants leg.

PIRATE

Requirements: a bright-colored shirt, black pants, a red sash and scarf, and boots.

Shirt and Pants

1. A ready-made shirt and pants can be used or you can make them from any basic pattern. Follow the instructions given with the patterns for assembling.

Sash

1. Cut a strip of red fabric about seven inches wide and long enough to tie around the waist. Turn under and stitch down a narrow hem on all sides.

Scarf

1. Cut a square of red fabric about twenty-two by twenty-two inches. Turn under and stitch down a narrow hem on all sides. Tie on head as shown.

COWBOY

Requirements: pants, a vest, a plaid shirt, a hat, and a bandana.

Vest

1. Use the bodice from any basic dress pattern. Lay the bodice back pattern on the fold of the fabric and cut it in one piece. Shape the bodice front as shown. Cut two back pieces and four front pieces.
2. Make darts and sew each pair of fronts together except at the shoulders and sides. Trim the seams, turn, and press. Do the same with the two backs.
3. Sew the back to the fronts along the shoulder and side seams.
4. Make fringe as described for Indian costume and sew all around the vest except for the armholes.

Pants

1. Use the pants from any basic pajama pattern. Follow the instructions given with the pattern for assembling.
2. Sew fringe along the sides of the pants legs.

Shirt

1. Use a ready-made shirt or make one with any basic shirt pattern. Follow the instructions given with the pattern for assembling.

Bandana

1. A ready-made bandana can be used or you can make one by cutting a square about the size of a man's handkerchief from bright fabric. Turn under and stitch down a narrow hem on all sides.

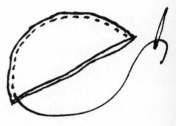

Hat

1. To make a pattern, measure around the head and add one inch. Draw a line half this length on paper. Shape as shown. Cut it out.
2. Using this as a guide, cut two pieces from fabric.
3. Sew the curved edges together. Trim the seam and turn.
4. To make the brim, draw a circle on paper the same size as the opening of the crown. Draw another circle five inches larger around this. Cut out as shown.
5. Using this as a guide, cut two pieces from fabric and one piece from brown paper.
6. Sew the pieces together with the brown paper in the middle. Trim the seam.
7. Attach the crown to the brim and stitch in place.
8. Sew fringe around the brim and where the crown joins the brim.

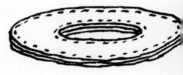

COWGIRL

Requirements: a skirt, a vest, a plaid shirt, a hat, and a bandana. (For the vest, shirt, hat, and bandana follow the same instructions as for the cowboy.)

Skirt

1. Use the skirt from any basic pattern. Cut it the length you want it to be.
2. Either gather the top and put a waistband on it or hem the top and insert elastic through the hem.
3. Turn under a narrow hem at the bottom of the skirt.
4. Make fringe as described for Indian costume and sew all around the bottom.

ANCIENT GREEK BOY

Requirements: a short tunic and a belt.

Tunic

1. The jacket of a pajama pattern can be adapted for this. Fold back the jacket front to the center line. Place this on the fold of the fabric. Mark the length you want the tunic to be. Cut as shown. Cut one front piece and one back piece.
2. Sew the side and shoulder seams.
3. Make a slit in the center of the back for a head opening. Bind the armholes and neck. Turn under and stitch down a narrow hem around the bottom.
4. Sew a snap or a hook and eye to the neck for fastening.
5. With crayon or felt pen make a Greek design around the hem and neck.

Belt

1. Cut a strip of fabric six inches wide and long enough to fit around the waist plus one inch. Turn under and stitch down a narrow hem on all sides.
2. Sew hooks and eyes at the end to fasten.
3. Decorate with the same design as the tunic.

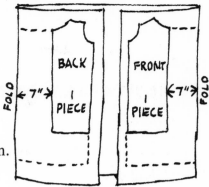

ANCIENT GREEK GIRL

Requirements: a long, loose-fitting gown.

Gown

1. Use the bodice from any basic dress pattern. Lay the pattern pieces seven inches from the fold. Mark the length that you want the gown to be plus two inches for the hem. Cut as shown.
2. Sew the side and shoulder seams.
3. Gather the neck to fit, then bind it.
4. Bind the armholes and hem the bottom.
5. Sew a snap or a hook and eye to the neck for fastening.

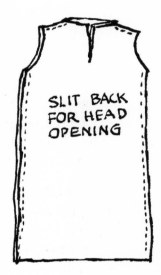

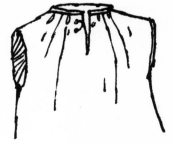

HAWAIIAN GIRL

Requirements: a grass skirt, a top, panties, and a lei.

Grass Skirt

1. Use a roll of crepe paper. About every half inch, slit the paper to within three inches of the width.
2. For the band, measure the waist plus one inch. Cut a strip of fabric this length and three inches wide. Fold the band in half lengthwise and press under a narrow hem along the edges.

3. Fold the crepe paper over itself until it is the length of the band. Slip the top of the crepe paper into the fold of the band and stitch in place.
4. Sew on hooks and eyes to fasten.

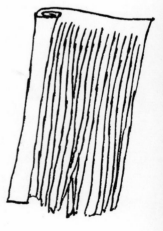

Panties

1. Use a panty or a short shorts pattern for this. Cut and assemble according to the instructions given with the pattern.

Top

1. The bodice pieces from any basic dress pattern can be used for this. Fold the back and front pieces to just above the natural waistline. Pin and cut two back pieces and one front piece from fabric.
2. Sew the front piece to the back pieces at the shoulder and side seams.
3. Turn under and stitch a hem along the sides of the back pieces. Close the back by sewing on snaps or using buttonholes and buttons.
4. Bind the armholes and neck. Turn up and stitch a hem around the bottom of the bodice. You may want to insert a piece of elastic through the hem to make the bodice fit more snugly.

Lei

1. Cut a strip of crepe paper about an inch and a half wide.
2. Thread a needle with enough heavy thread to make the lei the length you want it to be.
3. Gather the paper lengthwise through the middle.
4. Twist the paper around the thread until it gives the appearance of a series of circles.

33

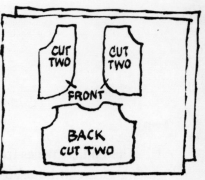

SPANISH BOY

Requirements: a black bolero, a white shirt, black-laced knee pants, a red or yellow belt, and a bandana.

Bolero

1. A pajama pattern can be adapted for this. Turn back the facing to the center front. Cut just below the natural waistline.
2. Sew each pair of fronts together except at the shoulders and sides. Turn and press. Do the same with the two backs.
3. Sew the back to the fronts at the shoulders and sides.
4. Set in the sleeves according to the instructions given with the pattern. Hem the sleeves.

Shirt

1. A ready-made white shirt can be used or make one from any basic shirt pattern.

Bandana

1. You can use a ready-made bandana or cut a square of fabric twenty-two by twenty-two inches. Turn under and stitch down a narrow hem on all sides.

34

Pants

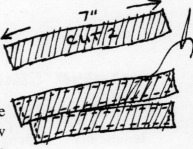

1. Use a pajama pants pattern. Cut the pants to just below the knees. Follow the instructions given with the pattern for assembling.
2. Cut two pieces of fabric seven inches long and three inches wide. Turn under and stitch down a narrow hem on all sides. Baste one piece to the side of each pants leg on the right side of the fabric. Stitch as shown. Cut between the stitched lines, turn, and press.
3. Either make six small buttonholes or set in six eyelets on each pants leg.
4. Starting from the top, lace the legs with black ribbon.

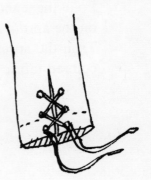

Belt

1. Cut a piece of fabric eight inches wide and long enough to fit around the waist.
2. Fold this piece lengthwise and stitch the long edge and one end together. Turn, stitch the open end, and press.
3. Sew on hooks and eyes to fasten.

SPANISH GIRL

Requirements: a long dress with a white bodice, a straight apron, a shawl, and a mantilla or kerchief.

Apron

1. Cut a strip of fabric the length and width you want the apron to be.
2. Turn under and stitch down a narrow hem on three sides.
3. Cut a strip of fabric about four inches wide and long enough to go around the waist and tie.
4. Turn under and stitch down a narrow hem on the sides and the ends.
5. Fold the band lengthwise. Center it on the apron, attach, and stitch.
6. Trim the apron with bands of bright-colored fabric or wide bias tape.

Dress

1. Any basic dress pattern will do. Cut
   the bodice out of white fabric. If you
   make the apron a bright color, make
   the skirt black, or vice versa. Cut the
   skirt the length you want it to be plus
   two inches for the hem. Follow the
   instructions given with the pattern for
   assembling.
2. Trim the skirt as you did the apron.

Shawl

1. You can use a ready-made shawl or
   cut a rectangle of fabric the size you
   want the shawl to be. Sew a line of
   stitching on all sides about three
   inches from the edge of the fabric.
   Make little slits every half inch or so
   from the edge to stitching line for
   fringe.

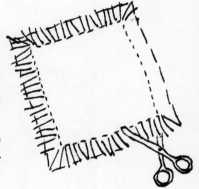

Head Covering

1. A large square of lace fabric will serve
   as a mantilla.
2. If you prefer a kerchief, a ready-made
   one may be used. Or you can cut a
   square of fabric twenty-two by
   twenty-two inches. Turn under and
   stitch down a narrow hem on all sides.

Holidays

Halloween

WITCH

Requirements: a long black dress, a black or orange cape, and a black pointed hat.

Dress

1. Use any basic dress pattern with long sleeves. Cut the skirt the length you want it to be plus two inches for the hem. Follow the instructions given with the pattern for assembling.

Cape

1. Fold the fabric with the selvages together. Starting from a corner, measure the length you want the cape to be. Measure the length from the same corner to the other points shown. Draw a curving line connecting these points. Cut along this line. Cut out a place for the neck.
2. Either bind the edges of the cape or turn under and stitch down a narrow hem.
3. Bind the neck, allowing enough binding on each end to make ties.

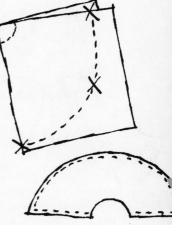

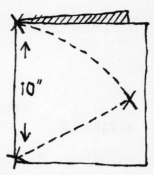

Hat

1. To make a pattern, measure around the head and add one inch. Draw a line half this length at an angle on a folded piece of paper. Draw another line ten inches above the first. Connect the lines as shown. Cut along the connecting line. Your pattern should be shaped like this.

2. Unfold pattern. Using this as a guide, cut one piece from fabric.

3. Sew the sides together and turn.

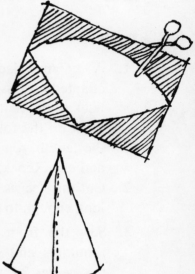

4. To make the brim, draw a circle on paper the same size as the opening of the crown. Draw another circle four inches larger around the first. Cut out as shown.

5. Using this as a guide, cut two pieces from fabric and one from brown paper.

6. Sew the pieces together with the brown paper in the middle.

7. Attach the crown to the brim and stitch in place.

GHOST

Requirements: a long tunic and a hood.

Tunic

1. A pajama jacket pattern can be adapted for this. Turn the jacket front back to the center line. Lay the jacket front on the fold of the fabric. Mark the length you want the tunic to be and cut. Repeat with back.
2. Cut the sleeves as shown. Make them long enough to cover the hands.
3. Sew the front to the back at the shoulders and sides. Make a slit in the center of the back for a head opening.
4. Bind the neck allowing enough binding at each end to make ties.
5. Set in and stitch sleeves.
6. Turn under and stitch down a narrow hem on the sleeves and the bottom.

SLEEVE
CUT
2

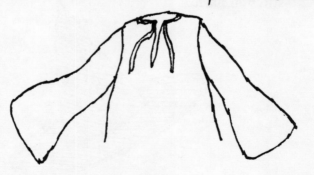

Hood

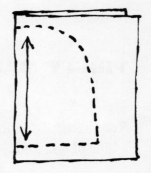

1. To make a pattern, measure from the top of the head to the shoulder. On a folded piece of paper draw a line this length. Shape as shown. Cut out and unfold.
2. Using this as a guide, cut two pieces from fabric.

3. Sew the curved sides of the pieces together. Trim the seams, turn, and press.
4. Turn under and stitch down a narrow hem around the bottom.
5. Cut out a place for the eyes, nose, and mouth in the front of the hood.

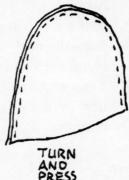

TURN AND PRESS

Christmas

VIRGIN MARY

Requirements: a long white gown, a sash, a blue cloak, and a headdress.

Gown

1. A long nightgown will make a pattern for this. Lay the gown on a double thickness of fabric. Cut around it leaving a margin for seams.
2. Stitch the shoulder and side seams. Clip the underarm seam so it will lie flat.
3. Make a slit in the back of the neck. Bind the neck allowing enough binding at each end to make ties.
4. Turn under and stitch down a narrow hem around the sleeves and the bottom.

Sash

1. Cut a strip of fabric four inches wide and long enough to tie comfortably around the waist.
2. Turn under and stitch down a narrow hem on all sides.

Cloak

1. Use a collarless robe pattern for this. Cut the sleeves fuller as shown. Follow the instructions given with the pattern for assembling, with the following exceptions:

    (a) Turn under and stitch down a hem about one-half inch wide around the sleeves, leaving a small opening. Insert elastic. Sew the ends of the elastic together and sew the opening.

    (b) Leave the front of the cloak open.

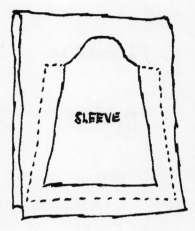

Headdress

1. Cut a square of fabric about thirty-two by thirty-two inches.
2. Turn under and stitch down a narrow hem on all sides.
3. Tie as shown.

ELASTIC

JOSEPH

Requirements: a long tunic and a sleeveless cloak.

Tunic

1. A buttoned-up bathrobe makes a good pattern for this. Lay the robe on a double thickness of fabric. Mark the length you want the tunic to be. Cut around the robe allowing a margin for seams. Cut a round neck.
2. Stitch the shoulder and side seams. Clip the underarm seams so they will lie flat.
3. Make a slit in the back of the neck. Bind the neck allowing enough binding at each end to make ties.
4. Turn under and stitch down a narrow hem around the sleeves and the bottom.

Cloak

1. From a contrasting fabric, cut a piece as long as the person is tall and the width of the fabric.
2. Turn under and stitch down a narrow hem on all sides.
3. Cut a strip of fabric about four inches wide and long enough to be tied comfortably around the waist.
4. Turn under and stitch down a narrow hem on all sides.
5. The cloak is draped over the left shoulder. The end hanging in back is carried diagonally across the back to the right hip. The sash holds the cloak in place.

SHEPHERD

Requirements: a loose-fitting robe with a sash or a rope tie, and a headdress.

Robe

1. A loose-fitting bathrobe makes a good pattern. Fold the closed robe length-wise and lay it on a double thickness of fabric. Add two inches to the center front. Cut, allowing for seams. Cut the sleeves fuller as shown. Repeat for back.
2. Sew the back pieces together down the center. Then sew the front pieces to the back.
3. Turn under two inches along the front. Stitch in place.
4. Bind the neck. Hem the sleeves and bottom.
5. Sew snaps at the neck to fasten.

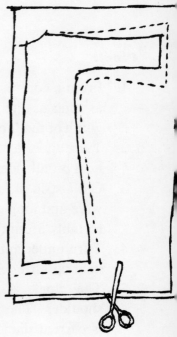

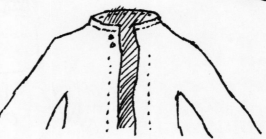

Sash

1. Cut a strip of fabric about thirty-six inches long and five inches wide. Turn under and stitch down a narrow hem on all sides.

Headdress

1. Cut a square of fabric about thirty-two by thirty-two inches. Turn under and stitch down a narrow hem on all sides. Tie as shown.

ANGEL

Requirements: a long-sleeved white gown, a halo, and wings (if desired).

Gown

1. Use the bodice from any basic dress pattern. Lay the pattern piece seven inches from the fold of the fabric. Mark the length you want the gown to be plus two inches for the hem. Cut one front piece and one back piece as shown.
2. Lay the sleeve pattern on a double thickness of fabric and cut as shown.
3. Sew the side and shoulder seams. Set in the sleeves according to the instructions given with the pattern and hem them.
4. Make a slit in the back of the neck. Gather the neck to fit. Bind it, allowing enough binding at each end to make ties.

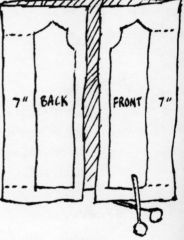

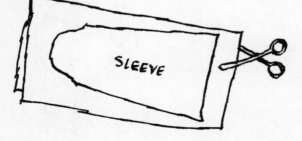

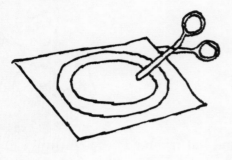

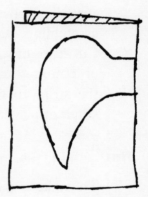

Halo

1. Cut a circle from cardboard the size you want the halo to be. Draw another circle one inch smaller inside the first. Cut this out.
2. Cut a piece of elastic long enough to fit comfortably around the head.
3. Make two small slits about an inch apart in the halo. Thread elastic through these slits and sew the ends together.
4. Paint the halo gold.

Wings

1. To make a pattern, use a folded piece of paper and draw the wings the size you want them to be, as shown. Cut and unfold.
2. Using this as a guide, cut two pairs of wings from fabric and one pair from brown paper.
3. Sew the wings together with the brown paper in the middle.
4. Paint the wings gold.
5. Pin or sew the wings to the gown where they should be.

SANTA CLAUS

Requirements: a red suit and hat trimmed with white, a black belt, boots, and a white beard.

Suit

1. A basic pajama pattern minus the collar is good for this. Follow the instructions given with the pattern for assembling. Bind the neck.
2. Cut strips of white terry cloth, flannel, or cotton three inches wide. Attach the strips to the coat as shown and stitch in place.

Hat

1. To make a pattern, measure around the head plus one inch. On a folded piece of paper draw a line half this length. Draw another line twelve inches above the first. Shape the pattern as shown. Cut it out and unfold.
2. Using this as a guide, cut one piece from red fabric.
3. Sew the sides together and turn.
4. Turn under and stitch down a narrow hem around the bottom.
5. Trim as shown with the same trimming used for the coat.

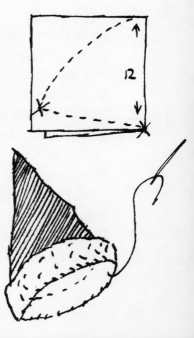

6. Sew two pieces of trimming together in a rounded shape. Turn and stuff. Or use a small ball of cotton. Attach to the hat as shown.

Belt

1. You can use a ready-made wide black belt or make one. In either case, have the belt large enough to go around whatever stuffing you may wish to use under the coat.
2. To make a belt, cut a strip of fabric eight inches wide and long enough to buckle around the waist.
3. Fold the belt in half lengthwise and stitch. Trim the seam, turn, and press. Tuck in the unsewn ends and sew.
4. Either attach a large buckle to the belt or fasten it in back and paint a large buckle on front.

Beard

1. Cut two pieces of fabric in the shape shown.
2. Sew the pieces together except across the top. Turn and press.
3. Bind the top, allowing enough binding at each end to make ties. If terry cloth or flannel is used, this completes the beard.
4. If cotton is used, glue the cotton to the cloth backing.

CHOIR BOY

Requirements: A white smocklike jacket with a big collar, and a bow tie.

Jacket

1. A pajama jacket pattern can be adapted for this. Fold the jacket front to the center line. Lay it on the fold of the fabric. Lay the jacket back on the fold also. Cut as shown.

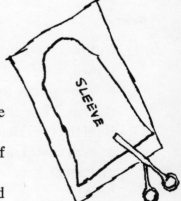

2. Lay the sleeve pattern on a double thickness of fabric. Cut as shown.
3. Sew the shoulder and side seams of the front and back together.
4. Sew the side seams of the sleeves and set them into the armholes.
5. Make a slit in the back of the neck.

6. To make a pattern for the collar, place the jacket on a piece of paper. Draw a line around the neckline from center front to center back. Remove the jacket. Shape the collar as shown. Cut it out.

7. Using this pattern as a guide, cut four pieces from fabric.

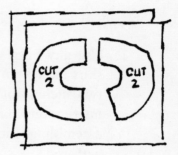

8. Sew each pair of pieces together except at the neck. Turn and press.

9. Fit the collars in place on the neck of the jacket, attach, and stitch.

10. Bind the neck, allowing enough binding at each end to make ties.

Bow Tie

1. Cut a long strip of black or red fabric about four inches wide.

2. Turn under and stitch down a narrow hem on all sides.

BACK

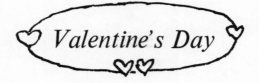

QUEEN OF HEARTS

Requirements: a white dress with red hearts and a heart-shaped hat.

Dress

1. Use any basic dress pattern. Cut the skirt the length you want it to be plus two inches for the hem. Follow the instructions given with the pattern for assembling. Bind the neck and sleeves with red.
2. From paper, cut a large heart pattern for the bodice front.
3. Using this as a guide, cut two hearts from red fabric. Sew them together, leaving a small opening for turning. Trim the seam, turn, sew the opening, and press.
4. Attach the heart to the bodice and stitch in place.
5. Following the same procedure, make smaller hearts and scatter them around the skirt.

TURN AND PRESS

Hat

1. Using the same size heart as for the bodice, cut two hearts from red fabric and one from brown paper.
2. Sew the hearts together with the brown paper in the middle. Trim the seams close to the stitching.
3. Cut a strip of fabric long enough to go around the head and make a bow under the chin.
4. Turn under and stitch down a narrow hem on all sides.
5. Attach the tie to the center of the heart and stitch in place.

Storybook Characters

MOTHER GOOSE

Requirements: a long red dress with a black, gray, or white drape, a black-laced bodice, a hat, and a cape lined with red.

Dress

1. Use any basic dress pattern. Cut the skirt the length you want it to be plus two inches for the hem. Follow the instructions given with the pattern for assembling up to the step for attaching the skirt to the bodice.

2. To make the drape, cut a width of folded fabric about three-quarters the length of the skirt. Shape as shown. Slit it about three inches down from the top along the fold.

3. Turn under and stitch down a narrow hem all the way around except for the top. Gather the top.

4. Starting at the center back, attach the drape to the skirt. Adjust the gathers so that there is a separation of about two inches at the center front. Stitch the drape in place.

5. Continue following the pattern instructions.

3" SLIT

Laced Bodice

1. Use the bodice from any basic dress pattern. Fold the bodice back to the center line. Lay it on the fold and cut in one piece. Shape the bodice front as shown and cut in two pieces. Cut two back pieces and four front pieces.
2. Make darts and sew each pair of fronts together except for the shoulder and side seams. Trim the seams, turn, and press. Do the same with the two backs.
3. Sew the fronts to the back at the shoulder and side seams.
4. Make four small buttonholes or use four eyelets on each side of the front bodice.
5. Starting at the top, lace the bodice with narrow black ribbon.

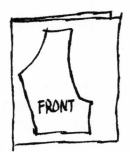

Hat

1. To make a pattern, measure around the head plus one inch. Draw a line half this length at an angle on a folded piece of paper. Draw another line about eight inches above the first. Connect the lines as shown. Your pattern should be shaped as shown. Cut along this line and unfold.

2. Using this as a guide, cut one piece from fabric.

3. Sew the sides together.

4. Cut a small circle to fit the top of the crown. Attach as shown and stitch in place. Turn.

5. To make the brim, draw a circle on paper the same size as the opening of the crown. Draw another circle four inches larger around the first. Cut as shown.

6. Using this as a guide, cut two pieces from fabric and one from brown paper.

7. Sew the pieces together with the brown paper in the middle.

8. Attach the crown to the brim and stitch in place.

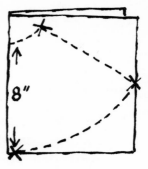

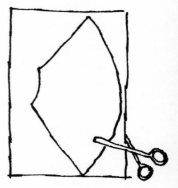

Cape

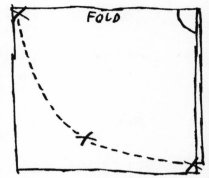

1. Fold the fabric as shown, with the selvages together. Starting from a corner, measure the length you want the cape to be. Measure the length from the same corner to the other points shown. Draw a curving line connecting these points. Cut along this line. Cut out a place for the neck.
2. Using this as a guide, cut another piece the same size for the lining.
3. Sew the two pieces together except at the neck. Turn and press.
4. Bind the neck, allowing enough binding at each end to make ties.

KING

Requirements: a long robe and a crown.

Robe

1. A loose-fitting bathrobe makes a good pattern for this. Fold the closed robe lengthwise and lay it on a double thickness of fabric. Add two inches to the center front. Cut, allowing a margin for seams and hems. Repeat for back. Cut the sleeves fuller as shown.
2. Sew the back pieces together down the center. Then sew the front pieces to the back at the shoulder and side seams.
3. Turn under two inches along the front. Stitch in place.
4. Bind the neck. Hem the sleeves and the bottom.
5. Sew snaps at the neck and along the front of the robe.
6. Sew on gold braid, fake fur, or some other trimming. Or you may wish to paint on gold trimming. If you do this, put paper between the layers of fabric as the gold paint quickly penetrates.

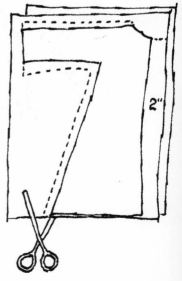

Crown

1. To make a pattern, measure around the head plus one inch. Draw a line half this long on a folded piece of paper. Draw another line five inches above the first.
2. Draw the pattern as shown. Cut it out and unfold.
3. Cut a piece of lightweight cardboard the length of the pattern. Trace the shape of the pattern on this. Cut this out.
4. Either paint the crown gold or cover it with gold paper.
5. Glue on bits of colored paper for jewels.
6. Staple the ends of the crown together.

5″

GLUE

PAINT

QUEEN

Requirements: a long-sleeved long dress, a contrasting overdress, a cloak, and a crown.

Dress

1. Use any basic dress pattern with long sleeves. Make the skirt the length you want it to be plus two inches for the hem. Cut a low round neckline. Follow the instructions given with the pattern for assembling.

Overdress

1. Use any basic dress pattern with short puffed sleeves. Make the skirt the length you want it to be plus two inches for the hem. Cut a low round neckline.
2. Split the skirt front down the middle. Turn back a two-inch hem on each side. Then follow the instructions given with the pattern for assembling.
3. Measure the width of the neckline and from the neckline to the waist plus one inch. Cut two pieces of fabric this size and shape as shown.

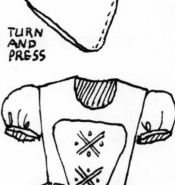

4. Sew the two pieces together, leaving a small opening for turning. Turn, sew the opening, and press.
5. Trim this piece as you like and attach it to the front of the overdress as shown. Stitch in place.

Cloak

1. Fold the fabric lengthwise. Measure the length you want the cloak to be and shape as shown.
2. Cut this out. If you want to line the cloak with a contrasting fabric, cut another piece the same size. Sew the pieces together except at the neckline. Turn and press.
3. If you choose not to line the cloak, turn under and stitch down a narrow hem all the way around except for the neck.
4. Bind the neck, allowing enough binding at each end to make ties.
5. Trim the cloak with terry cloth, cotton, or flannel to represent fur.

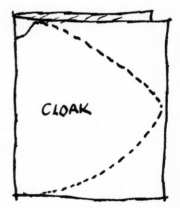

Crown

1. Follow the instructions for the king's crown.

LITTLE BO PEEP

Requirements: a long dress with a drape, and a bonnet.

Dress

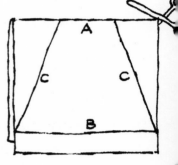

1. Use any basic dress pattern for this. Cut the skirt the length you want it to be plus two inches for the hem. Assemble the dress according to the instructions given with the pattern up to the step for attaching the skirt to the bodice.
2. To make the drapes, cut a piece of contrasting fabric the width of the fabric and the length of the skirt. Fold this piece in half and shape as shown. Cut along the fold to make two equal pieces.

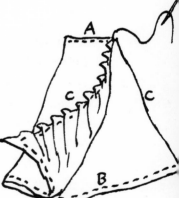

3. Fold line A in half with the right sides together. Stitch.
4. Turn under and stitch down a narrow hem along line B.
5. Open out and gather line C.
6. Starting at the center front, attach the gathered edge of the drapes to the bodice. Stitch in place.
7. Attach skirt to bodice. Turn the dress right side out. Bring the points of the

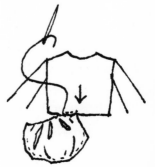

drapes to the side seams. Hand stitch in place.

8. Continue following the pattern instructions.

9. To make ruffles for the sleeves, cut two long strips from the fabric used for the drapes.

10. Turn under and stitch down a narrow hem along both sides. Gather each piece about one-half inch from the top.

11. Attach a ruffle to the edge of each sleeve and stitch in place.

Bonnet

1. To make a pattern, cut a piece of paper about ten inches wide and long enough to go around the head plus one inch. Round off the corners as shown. Cut this out.

2. Using this as a guide, cut two pieces from fabric.

3. Sew the pieces together, leaving a small opening for turning. Trim the seams, turn, sew the opening, and press.

4. Fit the bonnet around the head. Sew the ends in place.

5. Make a ruffle as for the dress. Attach the ruffle to the edge of the bonnet and stitch in place.

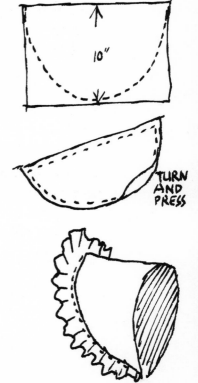

LITTLE BOY BLUE

Requirements: a blue suit, a bow tie, and a blue hat.

Suit

1. Use any basic pajama pattern for this. Follow the instructions given with the pattern for assembling.

Bow Tie

1. Cut a long strip of fabric about three inches wide.
2. Turn under and stitch down a narrow hem along the sides.

Hat

1. To make a pattern, measure around the head plus one inch. Draw a line half this length on paper and shape as shown. Cut this out.

2. Using this as a guide, cut two pieces from fabric.

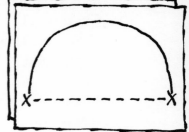

3. Sew the pieces together along the curved edges. Trim the seam and turn.
4. To make the brim, draw a circle on paper the same size as the opening of the crown. Draw another circle five inches larger around the first. Cut as shown.
5. Using this as a guide, cut two pieces from fabric and one from brown paper.
6. Sew the pieces together with the brown paper in the middle. Trim the seam.
7. Attach the crown to the brim and stitch in place.

TRIM AND TURN

5"

HANSEL

Requirements: a long-sleeved shirt, a sleeveless jacket, below-the-knee pants with suspenders, and a cap.

Shirt

1. Use a ready-made shirt or make one, using any basic shirt pattern. Follow the instructions given with the pattern for assembling.

Jacket

1. Use a pajama coat pattern. Omit the collar and sleeves. Follow the instructions given with the pattern for assembling. Bind the neck and armholes.

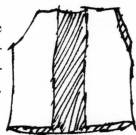

Pants

1. Use a pajama pants pattern. Fold the pattern to the length you want the legs to be plus an allowance for hemming. Follow the instructions given with the pattern for assembling.
2. Sew four buttons to the pants as shown for the suspenders.

Suspenders

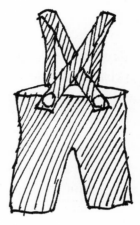

1. Cut two strips of fabric five inches wide and long enough to cross in back and fit comfortably over the shoulders.
2. Fold each strip lengthwise, right sides facing. Stitch the long edge and one end. Turn and press. Tuck in raw edges and stitch down.
3. Make buttonholes at each end of the straps.

Cap

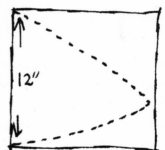

1. To make a pattern, measure the head plus one inch. Draw a line on a folded piece of paper half this length. Draw another line twelve inches above the first. Shape the cap as shown. Cut it out and unfold.
2. Using this as a guide, cut one piece from fabric.
3. Sew the sides of the cap together. Turn and press.
4. Turn under and stitch down a narrow hem around the bottom of the cap.

GRETEL

Requirements: a dress with a contrasting skirt and bodice, a laced bodice, and a cap.

Dress

1. Use any basic dress pattern, making the skirt of one color, the bodice of another. Cut the skirt the length you want it to be plus two inches for a hem. Follow the instructions given with the pattern for assembling.

Laced Bodice

1. To make a pattern, measure the waist. Draw a line half this length on a folded piece of paper. Draw another line nine inches above the first. Shape the pattern as shown. Cut it out and unfold.

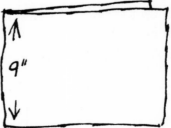

2. Using this as a guide, cut two pieces from black fabric.
3. Sew these two pieces together, leaving a small opening for turning. Turn, sew the opening, and press.
4. Either make four small buttonholes or use four eyelets on each side of the bodice.
5. For the straps, cut two strips of fabric two and a half inches wide and long enough to fit across the shoulders.
6. Fold each strip lengthwise, right sides facing. Stitch the long edge and one end, turn, and press. Tuck in the raw edges and stitch down.
7. Attach the straps to the bodice and stitch in place.
8. Lace the bodice with narrow ribbon.

Cap

1. Cut a piece of fabric fifteen inches long and eighteen inches wide.
2. Fold the piece in half lengthwise and stitch the edges together, leaving a small opening for turning. Turn, sew the opening, and press.
3. Sew the cap together as shown. Turn back about two inches to make the brim and tack it in place.

CINDERELLA

Requirements: a fancy long dress and costume jewelry.

Dress

1. Use any basic dress pattern. Cut the bodice with a low round neck. Cut the skirt the length you want it to be. Follow the instructions given with the pattern up to the step for attaching the skirt to the bodice.
2. Cut an underskirt from contrasting fabric.
3. Sew the sides of the underskirt together and gather the top. Turn under and stitch down a narrow hem around the bottom.
4. Cut strips of fabric about three inches wide for ruffles. Turn under and stitch down a narrow hem on both sides. Gather one side.
5. Sew two or three rows of ruffles on the bottom of the underskirt. Sew one ruffle around each sleeve.

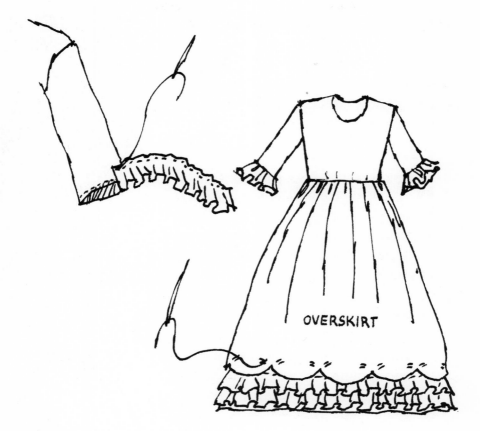

OVERSKIRT

6. Turn under and stitch down a narrow hem around the skirt. Attach the skirt to the bodice. Then attach the underskirt to the bodice. Stitch both skirts in place.

7. At intervals around the bottom of the skirt pleat as shown so that the underskirt ruffles will show. Hand stitch the pleats in place.

PRINCE CHARMING

Requirements: a coat, short bloomer-type pants, a neck ruffle, a beret-type hat, a cape, a narrow belt, and tights.

Coat

1. A pajama coat pattern can be used for this. Cut out the back, front, and sleeves.
2. Turn under and stitch down a narrow hem along the front facings. Stitch the facings in place. Turn and press.
3. Turn under and stitch down a narrow hem around the bottom of the front, the back, and the sleeves.
4. Sew bright strips of fabric or wide bias tape on the front and the sleeves.
5. Follow the instructions given with the pattern for assembling.
6. Sew bright strips of fabric or wide bias tape around the bottom of the coat, the neck, and the sleeves.

Pants

1. A pajama pants pattern can be adapted for this. Cut the pants just above the knee. Follow the instructions given with the pattern for assembling.
2. Insert elastic around the legs and the waist.

Neck Ruffle

1. Cut a long strip of lightweight white cotton fabric about three inches wide.
2. Turn under and stitch down a narrow hem on all sides.
3. Gather down the middle of the fabric. Make the ruffle long enough to fit comfortably around the neck.
4. Sew a snap at the end.

Hat

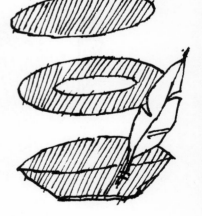

1. Cut two circles from fabric. From one circle, cut out a smaller circle, leaving a space large enough to fit around the head.
2. Sew the two circles together around the larger edge and turn.
3. Bind the head opening.
4. Sew a plume on one side of the beret.

Cape

1. Fold the fabric as shown, with the selvages together. Starting from a corner, measure the length you want the cape to be. Measure the length from the same corner to the other points shown. Draw a curving line connecting these points. Cut along this line. Cut out a place for the neck.
2. Using this as a guide, cut another piece the same size from a contrasting fabric for lining.
3. Sew the two pieces together except at the neck. Turn and press.
4. Bind the neck. Sew on a hook and eye for fastening.

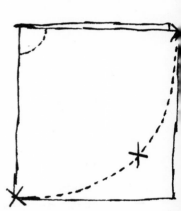

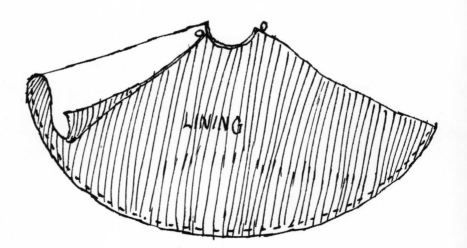

RED RIDING HOOD

Requirements: a red cape with a hood.

Cape and Hood

1. Fold the fabric with the selvages together. Starting from a corner, measure the length you want the cape to be. Measure the length from the same corner to the other points shown. Draw a curving line connecting these points. Cut along this line. Cut out a place for the neck.
2. To make a pattern for the hood, draw a line thirteen inches long on paper. Bisect it with a line eight inches long. Shape the hood as shown. Cut it out.
3. Using this as a guide, cut two pieces from fabric.
4. Sew the hood together as shown.
5. Turn under and stitch down a narrow hem along the front of the hood.
6. Attach the hood to the cape as shown.
7. Turn under and stitch down a narrow hem around the edges of the cape.
8. Sew on string ties at the neck.

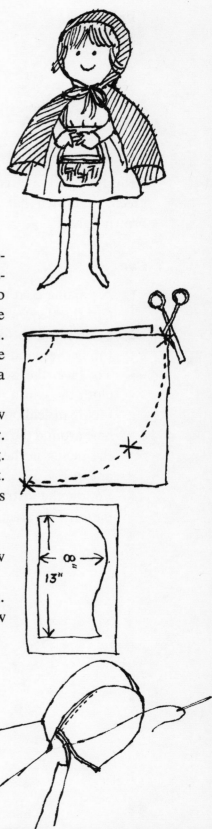

PETER PAN

Requirements: a green scalloped coat, a green or brown hat with a feather, and brown tights.

Coat

1. A pajama coat pattern is fine for this. Cut the sleeves short.
2. Scallop the bottom of the front, back, the sleeves, and the collar.
3. To face the scallops, cut strips of cloth the width of the scallop. Attach facing to scallops, right sides together. Sew around the scallops as shown. Cut the facing in the scallop shapes. Turn and press.
4. Follow the instructions given with the pattern for assembling.

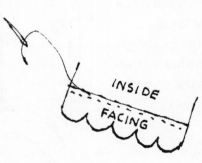

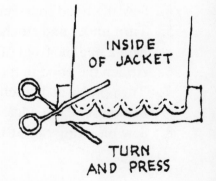

Hat

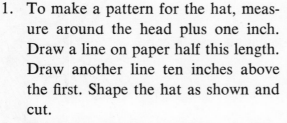

1. To make a pattern for the hat, measure around the head plus one inch. Draw a line on paper half this length. Draw another line ten inches above the first. Shape the hat as shown and cut.

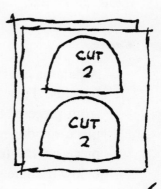

2. Using this pattern as a guide, cut four pieces from fabric.
3. Sew each pair of pieces together except at the bottom. Turn one pair.
4. With right sides facing, put one piece inside the other. Sew them together around the bottom, leaving a small opening for turning. Turn inside out and sew the opening. Tuck the lining inside the hat.
5. Fold back as shown to make a brim.

PIED PIPER

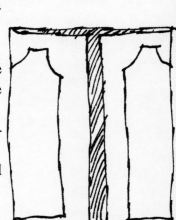

Requirements: a tunic with a sash, a cape, tights, and a hat.

Tunic

1. A pajama coat pattern can be adapted for this. Turn back the facing of the front piece to the center line. Lay the piece on the fold. Also lay the back piece on the fold. Cut as shown to a below-the-knee length.
2. Cut the sleeves.
3. Sew the front to the back at the shoulders and sides. Make a slit in the center of the back.
4. Set in the sleeves according to the instructions given with the pattern.
5. Bind the neck. Hem the sleeves and bottom.
6. Sew on a snap to fasten the neck.

Sash

1. Cut a strip of fabric four inches wide and long enough to go around the waist and tie.
2. Turn under and stitch down a narrow hem on all sides.

Cape

1. Fold the fabric as shown, with the selvages together. Starting from a corner, measure the length you want the cape to be. Measure the length from the same corner to the other points shown. Draw a curving line connecting these points. Cut along this line. Cut out a place for the neck.
2. Bind the edges or turn under and stitch down a narrow hem.
3. Bind the neck, allowing enough binding at each end to make ties.

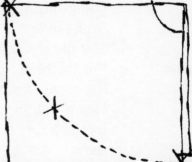

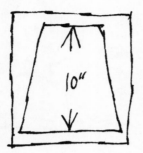

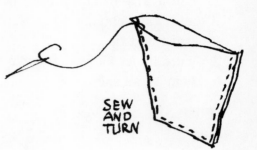

SEW
AND
TURN

Hat

1. To make a pattern, measure around the head plus one inch. Draw a line half this length on paper. Draw another line ten inches above the first. Connect the lines as shown. Cut this out.
2. Using this as a guide, cut two pieces from fabric.
3. Sew the top and sides together. Turn.
4. For the brim, draw a circle on paper the same size as the opening of the crown. Draw another circle three inches larger around the first. Cut as shown.
5. Using this as a guide, cut two circles from fabric and one from brown paper.
6. Sew the circles together with the brown paper in the middle. Trim the edges.
7. Attach the brim to the crown as shown and stitch in place.

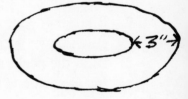

PINOCCHIO

Requirements: short suspender pants, a shirt with a large white collar, a bow tie, a vest, and a hat.

Pants

1. A pajama pants pattern is fine for this. Cut the legs the length you want them to be plus an allowance for hemming. Follow the instructions given with the pattern for assembling.
2. For the suspenders, cut strips of fabric about three inches wide and long enough to go across the shoulders comfortably.
3. Fold the fabric in half lengthwise and stitch. Turn, tuck in and stitch down raw ends, press.
4. Attach the suspenders to the back of the pants and stitch in place.
5. Make a buttonhole on the front end of each suspender. Sew buttons on the pants.

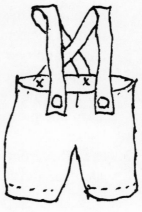

Shirt

1. A pajama jacket pattern can be adapted for this. Cut the sleeves short. Make the collar in the shape shown. Follow the instructions given with the pattern for assembling.

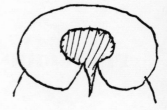

Bow Tie

1. Cut a strip of fabric about four inches wide and long enough to go around the neck and tie in a bow. Turn under and stitch down a narrow hem on all sides.

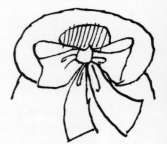

Vest

1. A pajama jacket pattern can be adapted for this as well. Fold back the front to the center line. Cut four front pieces and two back pieces.
2. Sew each pair of front pieces together except at the shoulder and side seams. Turn and press. Do the same with the backs.
3. Sew the fronts to the back at the shoulder and side seams.

Hat

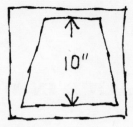

1. To make a pattern, measure around the head plus one inch. Draw a line half this length on paper. Draw another line ten inches above. Shape the hat as shown and cut.

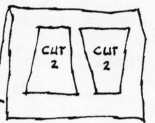

2. Using this as a guide, cut four pieces from fabric.
3. Sew each pair of pieces together except at the bottom. Turn one pair.
4. With right sides facing, put one piece inside the other. Sew them together around the bottom, leaving a small opening for turning. Turn, and sew the opening. Tuck the lining inside the hat.
5. Fold back as shown to make a brim.

ALICE IN WONDERLAND

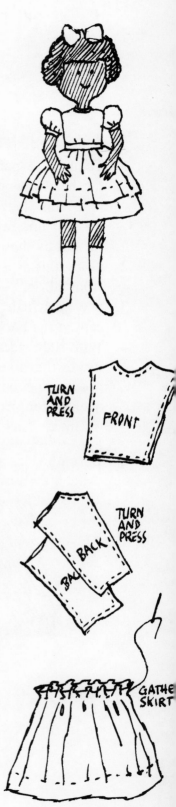

Requirements: a below-the-knee blue dress and a pinafore apron.

Dress

1. Use any basic dress pattern. Cut the skirt the length you want it to be plus two inches for a hem. Follow the instructions given with the pattern for assembling.

Pinafore

1. A basic dress pattern can be adapted for this. On the bodice front and back fold the pattern even with the widest part of the armhole. Cut two front pieces and four back pieces. Mark the length you want the skirt to be plus two inches for a hem, and cut it the width of the fabric.

2. Sew the front pieces together except at the shoulders. Trim the seams, turn, and press. Do the same for each pair of backs.

3. Sew the front to the back at the shoulders.

4. Sew the front and back of the skirt together. Gather the top of the skirt.

TURN AND PRESS

FRONT

TURN AND PRESS

BACK

BACK

GATHE SKIRT

5. For the skirt band, cut a strip of fabric about four inches wide and long enough to fit comfortably around the waist. Press under a narrow hem along the sides. Fold the band in half lengthwise.

6. Slip the skirt into the fold of the band and stitch in place.

7. Center the bodice on the skirt in the front and back. Attach the two together and stitch in place.

8. For the sashes, cut two strips of fabric about four inches wide and long enough to reach from the sides of the pinafore to the back and tie. Turn under and stitch down a narrow hem on both sides and one end.

9. Attach the unsewn ends of the sashes to the sides of the pinafore band. Stitch in place.

10. Make buttonholes and sew buttons at the back of the pinafore. Hem.

SNOW WHITE

Requirements: a long dress with a stand-up collar.

Dress

1. Use a dress pattern that buttons up the front, making the skirt of one color, the bodice of another, or adapt a basic dress pattern as follows. Fold the bodice back piece to the center line. Lay it on the fold and cut. Place the bodice front piece one and a half inches from the selvage and cut. Cut the sleeves. Mark the length you want the skirt to be plus two inches for a hem and cut it from a contrasting fabric. The skirt opening should be in the front.
2. Assemble the dress according to the instructions given with the pattern, adapting where necessary.

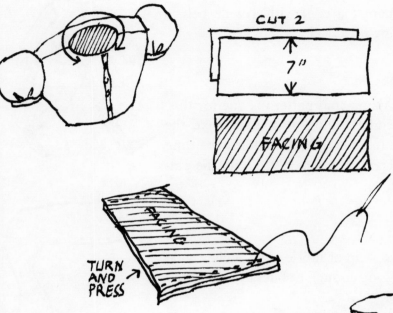

3. For the collar, measure from just in front of the shoulder seam on one side around the back to the same point on the other side. From white fabric cut two pieces that length and seven inches wide. Cut another piece the same size from a stiff interfacing.

4. Sew the interfacing and the white pieces together as shown. Turn and press.

5. Attach the collar to the neck and stitch in place. Face the neck edges.

DWARF

Requirements: a coat with a wide belt, a cap, and tights.

Coat

1. A pajama coat pattern is fine for this. Extend the cutting line to make the coat thigh length. Assemble according to the instructions given with the pattern.

Belt

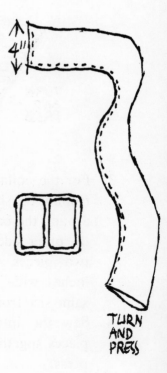

1. Cut a strip of fabric eight inches wide and long enough to buckle around the waist.
2. Fold the strip in half lengthwise and stitch. Trim the seam, turn, and press. Tuck in the unsewn ends and sew.
3. Either attach a large buckle to the belt or fasten it in back and paint a large buckle on front.

TURN AND PRESS

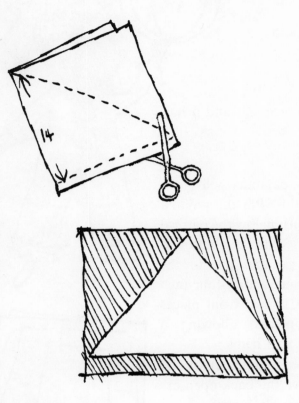

TURN
AND
PRESS

Cap

1. To make a pattern, measure around the head plus one inch. Draw a line half this length on a folded piece of paper. Draw another line fourteen inches above. Connect the lines as shown. Cut this out and unfold.
2. Using this as a guide, cut one piece from fabric.
3. Fold the piece and stitch it together except at the bottom. Trim the seam, turn, and press.
4. Turn under and stitch down a narrow hem around the bottom.

CLOWN

Requirements: a one-piece suit and a hat.

Suit

1. A pair of cotton pajamas will serve as a pattern for this. Pin the pajama pants to the coat just below the natural waistline. Then fold the buttoned pajamas lengthwise and pin to the fabric. (You will need forty-four-inch fabric for this.) Cut two front pieces and two back pieces, allowing a margin for seams and hems.

2. Sew the front pieces together at the center seam. Leave the back open except for the bottom six inches.

3. Sew the back to the front.

4. Turn under and stitch down hems around the arm and leg openings. Bind the neck.

5. For ruffles, cut long strips of fabric three inches wide. Turn under and stitch down a narrow hem on all sides. Gather down the middle of the fabric.

6. Sew ruffles around the neck, the sleeves, and the legs.

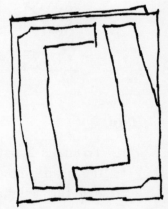

7. For pompoms, cut a three-inch square of cardboard. Wrap yarn around and around the cardboard. The more yarn you wrap the fuller the pompom will be. Slip a piece of yarn around the loops at one end and tie. Cut through the loops at the other end.

8. To fasten the back, use a zipper, hooks and eyes, or face it and use buttonholes and buttons.

Hat

1. To make a pattern, measure around the head plus one inch. Draw a line half this length on paper. Draw another line sixteen inches above the first. Join the lines as shown. Cut it out.

2. Using this as a guide, cut two pieces from fabric and two from brown paper.

3. Sew each pair of pieces together except at the bottom. Turn the fabric pieces.

4. Place the brown paper inside the fabric. Stitch around the bottom.

5. Put a ruffle around the bottom of the hat and a pompom on top.

16"

TURN

PAPER

SEW AROUND BOTTOM

FAIRY

Requirements: a dress with a long skirt of net or tarlatan, panties, and a ruffled head-band.

Dress

1. Use the bodice from any basic dress pattern. Cut two of the front bodice pieces and four of the back.
2. Make darts and assemble each of the two bodices.
3. With right sides facing, join the two bodices at the arm holes. Turn and press. Bind the neck and make button-holes in back.
4. Keeping the outer and inner bodices separated, turn under and stitch down a narrow hem all around.
5. Mark the length you want the skirt to be. Cut two pieces the width of the fabric. Leaving about four inches open at the top, sew each skirt together. Gather them at the top.

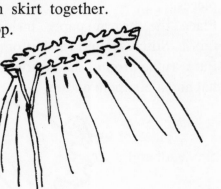

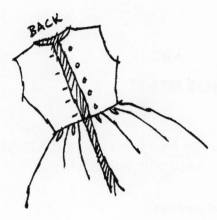

6. Attach the skirts in between the bodices with the opening in back. Stitch in place.
7. Sew on buttons.

Panties

1. Use any panty or short-shorts pattern. Cut and assemble according to the instructions given with the pattern.

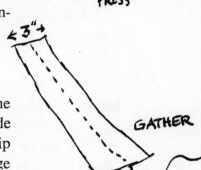

Headband

1. From the same fabric used for the bodice, cut a strip three inches wide and twelve inches long. Fold the strip in half lengthwise. Stitch the long edge and one end. Turn and press. Tuck in the unsewn edges and sew.
2. Cut a long strip of net three inches wide. Gather it down the middle.
3. Attach the ruffle to the band and stitch in place.
4. Sew a piece of elastic to the ends of the headband to make it fit.

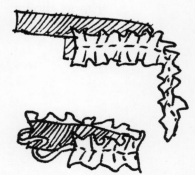

TOY SOLDIER

Requirements: blue pants and a red jacket
and hat trimmed with gold.

Pants and Jacket

1. Use a basic pajama pattern. Cut the
    jacket with a round neck. Follow the
    instructions given with the pattern for
    assembling.
2. Use gold buttons for the jacket. Sew
    on gold braid or use gold paint to trim
    the jacket as shown. (If you use gold
    paint, put paper in between the layers
    of fabric as the paint quickly pene-
    trates.)

Hat

1. Measure around the head plus one
    inch. Cut a piece of red fabric and a
    piece of brown paper this length and
    eleven inches high.
2. Sew gold braid or use gold paint to
    trim as shown.

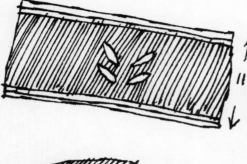

3. With the right sides facing, sew the fabric ends. Turn and press.

4. For the top, cut a circle of fabric the size of the head opening.

5. Attach the top to the sides as shown and stitch in place.

6. Fit the brown paper into the hat and stitch around the lower edge.

7. For the bib, draw on paper around the front edge of the hat. Using this line as a guide, draw the shape shown.

8. Cut one piece this shape from brown paper and two pieces from fabric.

9. Sew the pieces together with brown paper in the middle. Trim with gold braid or paint.

10. Attach the bib to the hat and stitch in place.

ELF

Requirements: a one-piece suit and a pointed hat.

Suit

1. A pair of cotton pajamas will serve as a pattern for this. Pin the pajama pants to the coat just below the natural waistline. Then fold the buttoned pajamas lengthwise and pin to the fabric. Cut two front pieces and two back pieces, allowing a margin for seams and hems.

2. Sew the front pieces together at the center seam. Leave the back open except for the bottom six inches.

3. Sew the back to the front.

4. Bind the neck. Turn under and stitch down narrow hems around the leg and arm openings.

5. To fasten the back opening you can use a zipper or hooks and eyes, or face the opening and use buttonholes and buttons.

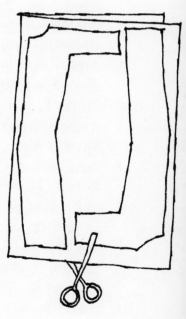

BACK

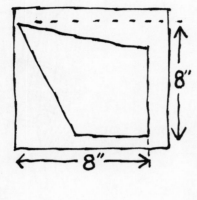

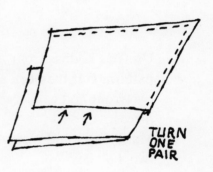

TURN
ONE
PAIR

Hat

1. To make a pattern, draw a line eight inches long on paper and another line eight inches long at the bottom of the first. Then draw the shape as shown and cut.
2. Using this as a guide, cut four pieces from fabric.
3. Sew each pair of pieces together as shown. Turn one pair.
4. With right sides facing, put one piece inside the other. Sew the pieces together around the front and bottom, leaving a small opening for turning. Turn, sew the opening, and press. Tuck the lining inside the hat.
5. Sew on string ties.

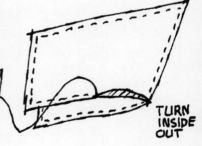

TURN
INSIDE
OUT

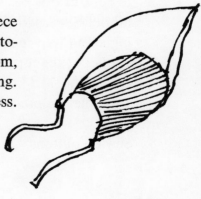

BALLET DANCER

Requirements: a dress with a short skirt of net or tarlatan, ruffled panties, and a ruffled hat.

Dress

1. Use the bodice from any basic dress pattern. Cut the neck a bit lower. Cut two front bodice pieces and four back pieces.
2. Make darts and assemble each of the two bodices.
3. With right sides facing, join the two bodices at the armholes. Turn and press.
4. Bind the neck and make buttonholes in back.
5. Keeping the outer and inner bodices separated, turn under and stitch down a narrow hem all around.
6. Mark the length you want the skirt to be. Cut two pieces the width of the fabric. Sew each skirt together, leaving about four inches open at the top. Gather at the top.
7. Attach the skirt in between the bodices with the opening in back. Stitch in place.
8. Sew on buttons.

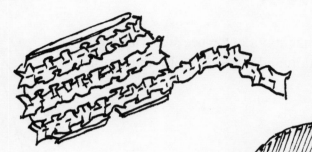

Panties

1. Use any panty or short shorts pattern. Cut and assemble according to the instructions given with the pattern.
2. For the ruffles, cut long strips of net about two inches wide. Gather the strips down the middle. Sew several rows of ruffles around the panties.

Hat

1. From the same fabric as the bodice, cut two small circles. Sew them together, leaving a small opening for turning. Turn, sew the opening, and press.
2. Cut a long strip of net about three inches wide. Gather it down the middle.
3. Attach the ruffle to the hat and stitch in place.
4. Sew on string or ribbon ties.

ANIMALS

Requirements: a one-piece suit with appropriate tail, and a hood with appropriate ears.

Suit

1. A pair of cotton pajamas will serve as a pattern for this. Pin the pajama pants to the coat just below the natural waistline. Then fold the buttoned pajamas lengthwise and pin to the fabric. (You will need forty-four-inch fabric.) Cut two front pieces and two back pieces, allowing a margin for seams and hems.
2. Sew the front pieces together at the center seam. Leave the back open except for the bottom six inches.
3. Sew the back to the front.
4. Turn under and stitch down hems around the arm and leg openings. Bind the neck.
5. To fasten the back opening you can use a zipper or hooks and eyes, or face the opening and use buttonholes and buttons.

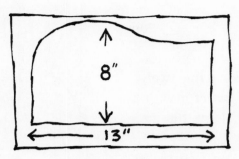

Hood

1. To make a pattern, draw a line about thirteen inches long on paper. Bisect it with a line about eight inches long. Shape the hood as shown and cut.
2. Using this as a guide, cut four pieces from fabric.
3. Sew each pair of pieces together as shown. Turn one pair.
4. With right sides facing, sew the pieces together, leaving a small opening for turning. Turn, sew the opening, and press. Tuck the lining inside.
5. Sew on string ties.

Rabbit Tail

1. Cut a three-inch square of cardboard. Wrap yarn around and around it. The more yarn you wrap the fuller the tail will be.
2. Tie a piece of yarn around the loops at one end. Cut through the loops at the other end.
3. Sew the tail in place on the suit.

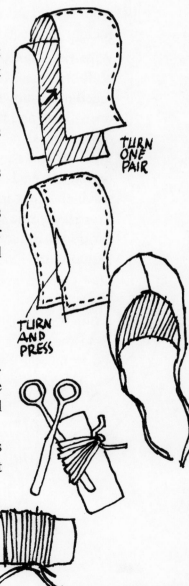

Rabbit Ears

1. To make a pattern, draw a line twelve inches long on paper. Bisect it with a line five inches long. Shape the ears as shown and cut.

2. Using this as a guide, cut four pieces from fabric and two from a stiff interfacing.

3. With right sides facing, sew one pair of fabric pieces and one interfacing together as shown, leaving the bottom open. Turn and press. Repeat with the other pieces.

4. Turn in the raw ends and fold the bottom of each ear as shown. Hand stitch the ears in place on the hood. From the inside of the hood, tack each ear about a quarter of the way from the bottom.

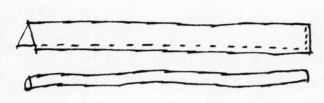

Mouse Tail

1. Cut a piece of bias tape the length you want the tail to be. Fold the tape in half lengthwise and stitch the long edge and one end. Turn and press.
2. Turn in the raw ends and hand stitch the tail in place on the suit.

Mouse Ears

1. To make a pattern, draw a line six inches long on paper. Bisect it with another line six inches long.
2. Shape the ears as shown and cut.
3. Using this as a guide, cut four pieces from fabric and two from a stiff interfacing.
4. With right sides facing, sew one pair of fabric pieces and one interfacing together as shown, leaving the bottom open. Turn and press. Repeat for the other pieces.
5. Turn in the raw ends. Hand stitch the ears to the hood from the front and then the back.

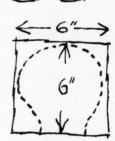

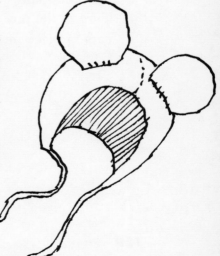

Dog Tail

1. Cut a piece of fabric about twenty inches long and five inches wide. Round it on one end.
2. Fold the fabric in half lengthwise and stitch the long edge and one end. Turn and press.
3. Stuff the tail.
4. Turn in the raw ends and hand stitch the tail in place on the suit.

Dog Ears

1. To make a pattern, draw a line ten inches long and bisect it with a line five inches long. Shape as shown and cut.
2. Using this as a guide, cut four pieces from fabric.
3. With right sides facing, sew one pair of pieces together except for the bottom. Turn and press. Repeat for the other pair.
4. Turn in the raw ends. Hand stitch the ears in place on the hood as shown.

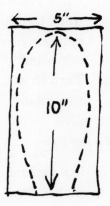

Cat Tail

1. Follow the same instruction as for the dog's tail.

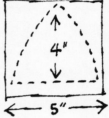

Cat Ears

1. To make a pattern, draw a line four inches long. Draw another line five inches long crossing the first at the bottom. Shape the ears as shown and cut.
2. Using this as a guide, cut four pieces from fabric and two from a stiff interfacing.
3. With right sides facing, sew one pair of fabric pieces and one interfacing together as shown, leaving the bottom open. Turn and press. Repeat for the other pieces.
4. Turn in the raw ends and hand stitch the ears to the hood from the front and then the back.